Your beautiful guide to living your best life

Blissed

Create your happiest life ever

Journal + Planner
2014

Marnie McDermott

Copyright © Marnie McDermott, 2014
www.marniemcdermott.com

All rights reserved. No part of this book may be used or reproduced or transmitted in any form or by any means, graphic, electronic, or mechanical, including photocopying, recording, taping or by any information storage retrieval system now known or to be invented without the permission of the publisher except in the case of brief quotations embodied in articles and reviews.

Illustration © Design on Q, 2014
www.designonq.com

ISBN 978 0 473 27252 4

See the range of inspiring books, journals and planners at www.gladileenmedia.com

CONTENTS

Dreaming   page 9

Doing   page 65

Believing   page 147

LOVE. HAPPINESS. BEAUTY. FULFILMENT. ABUNDANCE. JOY. PURPOSE.

These gifts – and more – are yours by right. Boundless. Just waiting for you to decide how richly, deeply and completely you will welcome them.

Something magical happens when you put pen to paper and let yourself dream.

You anchor your deepest wishes. You give promise to your heart. You bring meaning to your life.

You say "Yes" to your spirit. And such clarity allows every star in the Universe to whisper "Yes" in reply.

Come sweet soul, your beautiful life awaits.

How to use this journal

No matter where you are right now, this journal will carry you forward. Cradle you. Lift you to the next level.

It is your beautiful guide to your deepest truth and your happiest life.

It is the perfect blend of inspiration and implementation. It gives you permission to dream big, wish upon a star, and fall in love with your life. It will move you. It will uplift you. It will call you to focus. And to action. It allows you to open your arms wide to receive more of everything you desire. It will guide you to start living the life you truly want. Because that life, your truest life, will not happen by chance.

This journal guides you to see your life as it is, and as you want it to be. In its beautiful pages you can capture all your reflections, thoughts, hopes, dreams and promises to yourself. It's your all-in-one dream catcher, life planner and journal.

Here's how it works:

* **Start with the 'Dreaming'.** Connect with who you really are. Consider your hopes, dreams, loves, relationships, career, health, wellbeing and more. Use the questions as prompts to spark your thoughts and ideas.

* **Then anchor those dreams in the 'Doing'.** Know what you want, and set your focus every month to manifest all you desire with action and forward steps. Use the monthly planner, decide priorities, make lists, set timeframes, and watch your dreams unfold with ease.

* **Then you need to believe.** Believe in yourself. Believe you can do this. Believe you can bring your happiest life into being.

THE DECISIONS YOU MAKE IN EVERY MOMENT CREATE YOUR LIFE.

Dreams become reality because you make a choice.
A choice to love. To grow. To give. To embrace.

A choice to do something. Anything. One thing, every day, that takes you closer to your dream.

Now, turn off your pesky inner censor – there are no rights and wrongs here. All you have to do is dream.

Dream lofty dreams. Soul-tingling dreams.

Dream in colour. In full volume.
With every fibre of your being.

Let your beautiful life sparkle in your mind,
in your heart and on the page.

Give yourself permission to
DREAM BIG,
wish upon a star,
and fall in LOVE with YOUR LIFE

Dreaming

Your dreams need room to GROW

CREATE SPACE FOR THE NEW

To welcome goodness into your life, you must first create the space for it.

You need space to grow. Space for your soul to expand. Space for gifts to be received, wishes to be answered, dreams to breathe.

To create this space, start by reflecting on the year that has been.

Celebrate, give thanks and let go. By doing so, you become ready to embrace the new.

 Take time to reflect on the year that has been. Gather photos, your date calendar, your journal and other items that will help you remember all you have experienced over the past 12 months of your life. The questions on the following pages will guide you to create space for the new.

THE YEAR THAT HAS BEEN

What's changed in your life in the last year? What's new, better, different, clearer?

12 REASONS TO CELEBRATE

What do you want to celebrate about you?

BEAUTIFUL LESSONS. SOUL-STIRRING MOMENTS. SELF-DISCOVERIES. TRANSFORMATION.

1.
2.
3.
4.
5.
6.
7.
8.
9.
10.
11.
12.

12 MOMENTS TO TREASURE

What beautiful things happened during the year?

MEMORIES MADE. EXPERIENCES SHARED. SMILES IMPRINTED. HEARTS BURSTING. LOVE. JOY.

1.
2.
3.
4.
5.
6.
7.
8.
9.
10.
11.
12.

12 REASONS TO GIVE THANKS

What are you grateful for?

DREAMS REALISED. DESIRES MANIFESTED. FEARS CONQUERED. CHANCES TAKEN. GRATITUDE.

1.
2.
3.
4.
5.
6.
7.
8.
9.
10.
11.
12.

12 THINGS TO RELEASE

What do you need to let go of to create the space for your happiest life?

CHOICES MADE. WORDS SAID. DRAMAS UNFOLDED. REGRETS HELD. FEAR. WORRY. HURT.

1.
2.
3.
4.
5.
6.
7.
8.
9.
10.
11.
12.

MEDITATION

MAKE PEACE

Breathe and give thanks.
Fill your heart with beauty.
Celebrate all goodness that has passed.
Release with love all that cannot be undone.
Breathe and let go.
Arms open wide, say 'Yes' to life.
See the boundless flow of opportunity.
Embrace it. Nurture it. Watch it bloom.
Become light. Luminous. Shine.
All is beautiful. All is yours.
Perfectly. Divinely. Completely.
And so it is.

HAPPINESS
is saying
'YES'
to your spirit.

HAPPINESS IS WITHIN YOU

This whole journal is about realising your truest, happiest life. *Blissed* will guide you to dream, and make plans. But even with everything you ever wanted, you will only be happy when you get there if you know how to be happy right now.

Here's the key. Happiness is a present moment experience. Happiness is within you. And to be happy, you have to be deeply connected to *you*.

When you allow yourself to be happy for no reason at all – happy for life, happy for love, happy to let your soul smile – that's when you'll realise all the dreamy, glittering plans you had for your life have fallen into place right under your nose.

Your deepest happiness is never about what you have, or what you do. The more you open to your truest self, the more your light guides you home to the happiness that lies within you.

Remember, it's ok to have dreams and want good things. The key is to know how to be happy without them. They are not your source of happiness. You are.

 Use the following questions as prompts for understanding how you see happiness in your life right now, and how you can invite more present moment happiness into your life.

What feelings do you experience when you are happy?

How do you *want* your happiness to feel?

What creates the most joy in your life right now?

What insights do your answers to these questions bring?

THINK ABOUT YOUR LIFE.
HOW HAPPY AND CONTENTED DO YOU FEEL RIGHT NOW?

Record your level of happiness on the diagram below, and check in every month to track how you're feeling.

FIVE HAPPINESS CHOICES

I believe...

Happiness is a right not a reward.

Happiness is a daily choice.

I am my own happiness.

There is joy in the beautiful ordinary.

A balanced life is a happy life.

Conscious choices, repeated day after day, create our existence.
And you get the power to choose.

Be true, BE YOU.

THE YEAR AHEAD

Your gorgeous, happy, abundant year awaits. Now is the time to anchor your wishes, hopes and dreams.

When you take control of your life by setting clear intentions for what you want – and knowing why you want them – it's like all the resources of the universe align themselves to fill your orders. Thoughts become reality. Intentions become actions. Dreams grow.

Rather than racing ahead right now to what you want to *have*, or what you want to *do* this year, now is the time to pause. To connect with who *you* truly are. Because your truth is a magnet for the life of your dreams.

First ask yourself who you are. Then ask yourself how you want to feel in your life. Decide to make choices that allow you to truly be you. Do the things that help you feel how you want to feel. Only then will you live your truest, most fulfilling life.

 The following questions guide you to understand how you really want to feel, and to see how you can bring those desired feelings into your life.

WHO DO YOU WANT TO BE?

Who are you? Who do you want to be?

See all of your beautiful qualities and values. Note them in the space below. Aim for eight to ten core words that perfectly capture the essence of you. This is not about roles, jobs or titles. This is about who you really are.

KIND. LOVING. GENEROUS. PEACEFUL. JOYFUL. WISE. SPIRITED. PLAYFUL. BEAUTIFUL. DARING. CALM. CLEAR. HAPPY. COMPASSIONATE. COLOURFUL. CREATIVE. DETERMINED. GRACEFUL. GRATEFUL. BRIGHT. CURIOUS. GENTLE. TRUE. ROMANTIC. VIBRANT. PATIENT. GROUNDED.

Check in with this page as you work your way through this book and as the year ahead unfolds. When choices and opportunities present themselves, ask yourself, "If I do this, am I being true to me?" "Does this decision reflect who I really am?" "Am I being who I really want to be?"

HOW DO YOU WANT TO FEEL?

How do you most want to feel in your life?

Use the space below to get clear about the feelings, sensations and experiences that are most important to you. If you could choose the 10 best feelings to experience every day for the rest of your life, what would they be?

COURAGEOUS. INSPIRED. FREE. SUPPORTED. GENEROUS. LOVED. MINDFUL. SELF-FULL. NURTURED. SERENE. CONNECTED. DIVINE. EMPOWERED. ENERGISED. ENLIGHTENED. LIMITLESS. NOURISHED. TREASURED. WHOLE. SAFE. HAPPY. BLISSFUL. PROSPEROUS. GRATEFUL. BLESSED.

Check in with this page as you work your way through this book and as the year ahead unfolds. Ask yourself, "Will this make me feel how I want to feel?" "Does this decision reflect what's important in my life?" "Am I allowing myself to live the kind of life I really want to live?"

THIS YEAR

I most want to fill my life with...

I most want to experience...

I most want to enjoy...

I most want to love...

I most want to welcome…

I most want to give…

I most want to celebrate…

I most want to release/change…

LIFE.
Dream it.
Do it.
Love every moment of it.

YOUR HAPPIEST YEAR

Smile as you approach this part of your journal. This is where the magic begins. This is where you have freedom to pledge your deepest desires in each area of your life: purpose + spirit; lifestyle + living; love + relationships; health + wellbeing.

A balanced life is a happy life. It can be no other way. Like a glittering gem, we are multi-faceted beings. A beautiful life requires us to see the whole of our life, and to balance ourselves mind, body, emotion and spirit. This is where you set your intentions for your happy year, and your happy life.

We receive all we think we deserve. You deserve love, beauty and happiness. In abundance. Remember that, sweet soul.

Anchor your dreams

Over the following pages you will be guided to anchor your dreams across each of your four life areas: purpose + spirit; lifestyle + living; love + relationships; health + wellbeing.

* First, be grateful for what you love in each area of your life. What's working. And be aware of what is no longer serving you and needs to change.

* Then write your beautiful life story in each area. Your wishes for your life. Take the time to fully see, feel and experience your life as you want it to be. Write in the present tense. For example, start each statement with 'I am', as though everything you want is already real. Be detailed. Be expansive. Be expressive. Be boundless with all you desire and everything you wish for life.

* Then write a goal, affirmation or positive statement that summarises all you wish for in each part of your life. *Tip: Check in with pages 26 and 27 to be sure this is in alignment with how you want to be and what you want to feel.*

* Finally, in each area, decide one priority that will take you closer to your dream. It could be a 'to do', a focus, even a new belief about this part of your life. Just one key thing.

Once you've completed your plan, take a break. Allow the ideas, the awareness, the beauty of what you've created to infuse your heart and your whole being.

Come back to it in a few days. Check in. What's changed? What feels even clearer now? Refine it. Then start doing it.

This is where you make your life fizzy, gorgeous and blissful. Remember, it's up to you.

PURPOSE + SPIRIT

This is the most important part of your life. It relates to your deepest self. It's about how you express yourself. How you show up in the world. How you ensure you are your best you, so you can help others be their best too. It's about trust in yourself. Acceptance of yourself. It's about who you are.

I love…
What are you grateful for? What's working? What do you want more of?

I release…
What's not working? What do you no longer need? What needs to stop?

Life Dreams

Dreams are like soul-food. They connect us to our truest self and our deepest desires. Whether big or small, they give us purpose. By saying 'Yes' to our dreams, we say 'Yes' to ourselves. What are *your* dreams? If you could be, do or have anything, what would it be? When do you feel most on purpose, or connected or in the flow?

Wishes for my life:

My dreams

Short-term (1-3 years)

GOAL / AFFIRMATION: _____

MY ONE KEY THING: _____

Medium-term (5 years)

GOAL / AFFIRMATION: _____

MY ONE KEY THING: _____

Long-term (10 Years)

GOAL / AFFIRMATION: _____

MY ONE KEY THING: _____

Meaning

Our values, beliefs and passions give life its deepest meaning. When we live in alignment with these innermost parts of ourselves, we can't help but be on purpose and filling our life with happiness and contentment.

What do you believe in?

What do you value?

What will you never do?

GOAL / AFFIRMATION: _____

MY ONE KEY THING: _____

LIFESTYLE + LIVING

This relates to all aspects of your career and finances, education, and lifestyle factors like your home, possessions and travel. It's about what you do and what you have.

I love…
What are you grateful for? What's working? What do you want more of?

I release…
What's not working? What do you no longer need? What needs to stop?

Home

Your home is your sanctuary. The spaces in your life not only reflect who you are, they can nourish or drain you too. Small changes and an ordered approach to every space in your life – be it home, office, car, or handbag(!) – can free your energy and your time. Do you want to move or are you happy where you are? How do you want your home or your space to feel? Is it inviting? Warm? Does it have a sense of space and light? How can you love it more? How can it support you more?

Dreams for my home:

GOAL / AFFIRMATION: _____

MY ONE KEY THING: _____

Dreams for other spaces in my life:

GOAL / AFFIRMATION: _____

MY ONE KEY THING: _____

Career

For most of us work, business, or study takes up much of our time, energy and focus. The ultimate goal is to combine your purpose and passion with the thing you do every day. That's when you feel the most happy and content. Are you doing what you truly love? What are your career, business or study goals? How are you learning and growing? Where do you want to be and how can you get there? Are you earning what you're worth?

Dreams for my career:

GOAL / AFFIRMATION: _____

MY ONE KEY THING: _____

Experiences

We are designed to experience our lives through all of our senses. We yearn for colour, magic, even adventure to feed our spirits. How are you feeding yourself with new experiences and situations? What new things do you want to try or explore? Where would you love to travel to or visit this year?

Dream experiences to create:

GOAL/AFFIRMATION: _____

MY ONE KEY THING: _____

LOVE + RELATIONSHIPS

This is about the love in your life. Love for yourself, love for others, love for your community and the planet. It's about how you nurture others and cherish yourself. It's about how you connect, engage and express. Heart to heart, soul to soul.

I love…
What are you grateful for? What's working? What do you want more of?

I release…
What's not working? What do you no longer need? What needs to stop?

You

You are the most important relationship you will ever have and giving to yourself is a self-full gift. An essential act. Remember, being selfless serves no one, least of all you. How will you celebrate and treasure yourself? How do you want to spend your birthday? What is your self-love mantra for the year? What do you want to do for you? How will you be more gentle and kind to yourself? How will you be a better friend to you?

This year I treasure myself by...

GOAL / AFFIRMATION:

MY ONE KEY THING:

Your Partner, Family + Friends

Life is enriched by the people we love, and who love us. You deserve to be surrounded by people who cherish you, believe in you, and sing the song of your heart to you when you have forgotten its tune. Is your circle full of people who love, nurture and support you? How do you treasure those in your life? How will you be a better friend to others? How can you create more memories and experiences together? What relationship patterns do you need to release? Are you ready to call in your soul love?

This year I treasure others by...

GOAL / AFFIRMATION: _____

MY ONE KEY THING: _____

Your Community

World happiness starts with you. Just one small act can create a ripple of goodness in your community. You can make the world a better place through simple, thoughtful action. How can you help others? How can you give to your community? Can you be more friendly with your neighbours? Clean up a local park? Volunteer at an animal shelter? How will you make a contribution and spread love and light?

This year I give to others by...

GOAL / AFFIRMATION:

MY ONE KEY THING:

HEALTH + WELLBEING

This is about your physical self. Your health, nutrition, self-care, as well as leisure activities, hobbies and relaxation. It's about how you nourish, support and renew yourself.

I love…
What are you grateful for? What's working? What do you want more of?

I release…
What's not working? What do you no longer need? What needs to stop?

Health

Health and happiness are intertwined. Good health enables you to be more balanced. And balance allows your beautiful life to flow with ease. Think about health, nutrition, heart-thumping movement. How do you feel about yourself? How do you want to feel? Do you get enough sleep? Drink enough water? Eat foods that nourish you? What are your exercise goals? Are you up-to-date with health check-ups? What would your healthiest life look like? How can you love the physical you even more?

My healthy life is:

GOAL / AFFIRMATION:

MY ONE KEY THING:

Fun + Play

Sometimes we treat the things we love to do as a reward that we have to earn, rather than an essential part of our life. What do you love? How do you have fun? What are you passionate about? What new things do you want to try? How often do you want to indulge your interests or hobbies?

My fun times are:

GOAL / AFFIRMATION: _____

MY ONE KEY THING: _____

Rest + Relaxation

Inevitably, life can become busy. When we're on the go, finding the time to rest and recharge can be tricky. How do you like to relax? How peaceful, centred and balanced do you want to feel in your life? How can you give yourself more essential 'you' time? How can you bring more calm energy into your life?

Me time this year looks like:

GOAL / AFFIRMATION: _____

MY ONE KEY THING: _____

101 THINGS – to try, experience, love, enjoy, savour, share, do, tick-off, remember...

Think of this as your bucket list for the coming year and beyond. A place to anchor all those ideas and must-dos that swim around in your head. A place for little moments to have big impacts. Your wishlist for the year. Come back to it throughout the year. Add to it, amend if necessary, and check off with glee all that has materialised.

TRY A NEW RECIPE EVERY WEEK. JOIN A MEDITATION GROUP. WATCH THE SUNRISE. START YOGA. GROW A VEGETABLE GARDEN. LEARN SPANISH. SAVE FOR A HOLIDAY. GO TO BED BY 10PM NIGHTLY. LIMIT TV TIME. UPGRADE MY PHONE. SET A BUDGET. JOURNAL DAILY. GET ORACLE CARDS. ORGANISE MY OFFICE. TREAT MYSELF TO FRESH FLOWERS. START MY OWN BUSINESS.

THE BLISS LIST

By now you will be brimming with ideas. Filled with possibilities. And starting to draw goodness to you for the year ahead.

Now's the time to get really specific. Read back over the pages you have completed. What's on your A-list? What's so exciting it makes you fizz? What feels deeply important? What feels like the time is now? What do you just have to do? What are your dreamiest dreams that just can't wait a moment longer? What resonates with who you want to be and how you want to feel in your life?

Try and come up with a list of your top 10-12 priority goals for the year ahead. Maybe you will only have 3-4. Whatever you do, trust it's perfect for you. This is your Bliss List, your main focus for the year to come.

To ensure every part of your life is in balance, so that love, happiness and abundance flows with ease, try to have a goal in every part of your life.

MY BLISS LIST

PURPOSE + SPIRIT	Purpose	Meaning	
LIFESTYLE + LIVING	Home	Career	Experiences
LOVE + RELATIONSHIPS	Me	Family + Friends	Community
HEALTH + WELLBEING	Health	Fun + Play	Rest + Relaxation

BLISS LIST STEPPING STONES

The world's most successful people have one thing in common: they know what they want, they have a plan to get there, and they put one foot in front of the other. Simple.

Your beautiful life is closer than you think. The amazing year that you dream of can so easily become more than just a dream. When you create a series of stepping stones and simply start moving, every step takes you from dream to reality.

Now's the time to break down each goal on your Bliss List. To make it achievable, tangible, and do-able.

 Remember, each goal will become a focus for one month of the year. Or maybe you can tick off two goals in one month, while another will span two months. Be flexible. Do what works for you.

There are only two ingredients in the life of your dreams:
The DREAMING and the DOING.

BLISS LIST STEPPING STONES

JANUARY

Goal:

Stepping stones:

1.
2.
3.
4.

FOCUS / GUIDING WORD / FEELING

FEBRUARY

Goal:

Stepping stones:

1.
2.
3.
4.

FOCUS / GUIDING WORD / FEELING

MARCH

Goal:

Stepping stones:

1.
2.
3.
4.

FOCUS / GUIDING WORD / FEELING

APRIL

Goal:

Stepping stones:

1.
2.
3.
4.

FOCUS / GUIDING WORD / FEELING

BLISS LIST STEPPING STONES

MAY

Goal:

Stepping stones:

1.
2.
3.
4.

FOCUS / GUIDING WORD / FEELING

JUNE

Goal:

Stepping stones:

1.
2.
3.
4.

FOCUS / GUIDING WORD / FEELING

JULY

Goal:

Stepping stones:

1.
2.
3.
4.

FOCUS / GUIDING WORD / FEELING

AUGUST

Goal:

Stepping stones:

1.
2.
3.
4.

FOCUS / GUIDING WORD / FEELING

BLISS LIST STEPPING STONES

SEPTEMBER

Goal:

Stepping stones:

1.
2.
3.
4.

FOCUS / GUIDING WORD / FEELING

OCTOBER

Goal:

Stepping stones:

1.
2.
3.
4.

FOCUS / GUIDING WORD / FEELING

NOVEMBER

Goal:

Stepping stones:

1.
2.
3.
4.

FOCUS / GUIDING WORD / FEELING

DECEMBER

Goal:

Stepping stones:

1.
2.
3.
4.

FOCUS / GUIDING WORD / FEELING

Dream. BIG.

Your year in a word

Let all your dreams sit with you. All the lists. All the words. All the ideas you have had about your beautiful life. Summarise it all into one beautiful word. A powerful intention. A divine magnet for your dreams. An anchor for your focus. The beacon to your true north. A theme for your amazing year. What would it be?

2014, MY YEAR OF...

ME. TRANSFORMATION. AWAKENING. CONSOLIDATION. FREEDOM. LOVE. BEAUTY. HOPE. BELIEF. ACCEPTANCE. CHANGE. JOY. BRIGHTNESS. RELEASING. DETOXING. NOURISHING. HEALING. LEARNING. GROWING. BUILDING. BEGINNINGS. ENDINGS. CREATION. BEING. KNOWING.

Everything I dream of comes to me with **EASE AND GRACE.**

DREAM IN COLOUR
Vision Board

I am open to receiving my heart's desires. I deserve goodness. Everything I dream of comes to me with ease and grace. And so it is.

Use pictures, words, images, doodles or sketches to capture your dreams for your beautiful life this year and beyond. Use your word for the year as an anchor.

Happiness is in EVERY breath and EVERY moment.

MY DAILY HAPPINESS HABITS

The key ingredient in your dream life is you. It's your energy that makes your life all you dream it to be. Nothing happens without beautiful, gorgeous, courageous you!

So, think about the everyday things you absolutely love. The things that light you up and lift your spirit. The things that help you feel more content, peaceful and centred in your day. Think back to the way you want to be, and the way you want to feel in your life. What new habits do you need to help you feel that way?

These are your essential rituals for feeling good; your daily happiness habits. List them now.

* _____
* _____
* _____
* _____
* _____
* _____
* _____
* _____

MEDITATE. EARLY TO BED, EARLY TO RISE. KEEP HYDRATED. HAVE TV-FREE NIGHTS. EXERCISE FOR 60 MINUTES. READ. GET FRESH AIR. BREATHE. CHOOSE POSITIVITY. ONLY EAT WHAT NOURISHES ME. WRITE. BE GRATEFUL. FRESH FLOWERS. WALKS. YOGA. JOURNAL. ME TIME.

MEDITATION

WELCOME HAPPINESS

*Breathe deeply. Draw in peace.
Bathe in blissful energy. Relax.
Release all heaviness from your heart.
Let worry, fear and regret float gently away.
Love heals you. Purifies you. All is well.
Life's delicate wonder and beauty infuses you.
Give thanks. Allow gifts to bless you, always.
Open your heart to you. All of you.
Feel the radiance of your true essence.
Let divine love nourish your spirit.
You are love. You are joy. You are happiness.
Abundantly. Eternally. Beautifully.
And so it is.*

HAPPINESS
is an expression of the soul in considered actions.

Doing

HAPPINESS STARTS TODAY

Happy days create beautiful weeks.

Beautiful weeks make gorgeous months.

Gorgeous months grow amazing years.

Amazing years add up to a lifetime of bliss.

MANIFESTING YOUR DREAM LIFE

Want to know the secret to manifesting your dream life? Simple. First align your inner and outer worlds, and then bring ordered flow to your life.

Through these pages you have set your deepest intentions for your life. Now, align with them. Heart and mind. Body and soul. Inner and outer. Walk the talk. Decide you deserve this goodness. And watch it bloom.

You can gauge your alignment by noticing what happens in your heart (feelings) and your mind (thoughts) when you think about your dreamiest intentions and goals. For each one you've chosen, ask yourself:

* Do I truly believe in myself?
* Do the actions in my life say 'I want this'?
* How can I align my head and my heart with my desires?

Then, to get serious about syncing your inner and outer life, create order. Order helps everything flow with focused action. And good habits get you where you want to be, faster. Manifesting your dream life through perfect order looks like this:

Yearly: **DREAM**	Plan an annual soulful retreat. Use your *Blissed* planner for crystal clear clarity on your dreams and desires.
Quarterly: **CHECK-IN**	Have a mini retreat every quarter to pause, reconnect, refocus and keep in flow.
Monthly: **PLAN**	Map out the month ahead. Know what you need to do (actions), and when you need to do it by (timeframes).
Weekly: **ACT**	Plan the week ahead. Bring dreams into being with simple, achievable, bite-sized steps.
Daily: **FOCUS**	Try a daily intention or mini mantra to keep you focused on how you want to feel, or what you want to achieve.

When you move from dreaming to doing, you attract all the creative forces of the universe. Anything becomes possible. Allow yourself to express who you truly are in the world and prepare to be delighted, amazed and blessed.

 # MY WEEKLY PLANNER

Week of:

Monthly Goals

Weekly Goals

Making it happen

MON

TUE

WED

THUR

FRI

SAT

SUN

Visit **www.marniemcdermott.com** to print this checklist for daily use.

JANUARY

Impossible becomes possible the moment you believe you can.

JANUARY

MONDAY	TUESDAY	WEDNESDAY	THURSDAY	FRIDAY	SATURDAY	SUNDAY
		1	2	3	4	5
6	7	8	9	10	11	12
13	14	15	16	17	18	19
20	21	22	23	24	25	26
27	28	29	30	31		

Check back on your Bliss List goals, stepping stones, and your 101 Things list. What are you going to make a priority this month? What will you do to take you a step closer to where you want to be? Is there anything new you need to add this month?

My Goals	By When?	Done ✓

Am I in alignment with these goals?

What may block me achieving them this month, and what I can do about it?

What resources or help will I need?

Use this page to note all the little things, and the big things that you need to do, remember, schedule or make time for this month.

Things to Do:

Things to Remember / Schedule:

Ways to Treasure Myself:

MONTHLY MANIFESTATION

What do you want to create in your life this month? A pay rise, a proposal, an unexpected gift, a new soulful friend, new shoes, a green smoothie, a parking space at work? Have fun with it. Remember, the universe delights in bringing you gifts. But first, you must place your order. Do so here. Be as specific as you can: the more detail you use, the more you fine-tune your ability to attract all you desire.

MY BLISSED MONTH ORDER

EVERYTHING I'M GRATEFUL FOR THIS MONTH

FEBRUARY

Take action to create the life you want. Simple.

FEBRUARY

MONDAY	TUESDAY	WEDNESDAY	THURSDAY	FRIDAY	SATURDAY	SUNDAY
					1	2
3	4	5	6	7	8	9
10	11	12	13	14	15	16
17	18	19	20	21	22	23
24	25	26	27	28		

Check back on your Bliss List goals, stepping stones, and your 101 Things list. What are you going to make a priority this month? What will you do to take you a step closer to where you want to be? Is there anything new you need to add this month?

My Goals	By When?	Done ✓

Am I in alignment with these goals?

What may block me achieving them this month, and what I can do about it?

What resources or help will I need?

Use this page to note all the little things, and the big things that you need to do, remember, schedule or make time for this month.

Things to Do:

Things to Remember / Schedule:

Ways to Treasure Myself:

MONTHLY MANIFESTATION

What do you want to create in your life this month? A pay rise, a proposal, an unexpected gift, a new soulful friend, new shoes, a green smoothie, a parking space at work? Have fun with it. Remember, the universe delights in bringing you gifts. But first, you must place your order. Do so here. Be as specific as you can: the more detail you use, the more you fine-tune your ability to attract all you desire.

MY BLISSED MONTH ORDER

EVERYTHING I'M GRATEFUL FOR THIS MONTH

MARCH

The only thing to do in life is the thing that says yes to your soul.

MARCH

MONDAY	TUESDAY	WEDNESDAY	THURSDAY	FRIDAY	SATURDAY	SUNDAY
31					1	2
3	4	5	6	7	8	9
10	11	12	13	14	15	16
17	18	19	20	21	22	23
24	25	26	27	28	29	30

Check back on your Bliss List goals, stepping stones, and your 101 Things list. What are you going to make a priority this month? What will you do to take you a step closer to where you want to be? Is there anything new you need to add this month?

My Goals	By When?	Done

Am I in alignment with these goals?

What may block me achieving them this month, and what I can do about it?

What resources or help will I need?

Use this page to note all the little things, and the big things that you need to do, remember, schedule or make time for this month.

Things to Do:

Things to Remember / Schedule:

Ways to Treasure Myself:

MONTHLY MANIFESTATION

What do you want to create in your life this month? A pay rise, a proposal, an unexpected gift, a new soulful friend, new shoes, a green smoothie, a parking space at work? Have fun with it. Remember, the universe delights in bringing you gifts. But first, you must place your order. Do so here. Be as specific as you can: the more detail you use, the more you fine-tune your ability to attract all you desire.

MY BLISSED MONTH ORDER

EVERYTHING I'M GRATEFUL FOR THIS MONTH

APRIL

You are not comparable to anyone else.
Be your own North Star.
Allow yourself to truly shine.

APRIL

MONDAY	TUESDAY	WEDNESDAY	THURSDAY	FRIDAY	SATURDAY	SUNDAY
	1	2	3	4	5	6
7	8	9	10	11	12	13
14	15	16	17	18	19	20
21	22	23	24	25	26	27
28	29	30				

Check back on your Bliss List goals, stepping stones, and your 101 Things list. What are you going to make a priority this month? What will you do to take you a step closer to where you want to be? Is there anything new you need to add this month?

My Goals	By When?	Done ✓

Am I in alignment with these goals?

What may block me achieving them this month, and what I can do about it?

What resources or help will I need?

Use this page to note all the little things, and the big things that you need to do, remember, schedule or make time for this month.

Things to Do:

Things to Remember / Schedule:

Ways to Treasure Myself:

MONTHLY MANIFESTATION

What do you want to create in your life this month? A pay rise, a proposal, an unexpected gift, a new soulful friend, new shoes, a green smoothie, a parking space at work? Have fun with it. Remember, the universe delights in bringing you gifts. But first, you must place your order. Do so here. Be as specific as you can: the more detail you use, the more you fine-tune your ability to attract all you desire.

MY BLISSED MONTH ORDER

EVERYTHING I'M GRATEFUL FOR THIS MONTH

MAY

*Truth lives in your heart.
Not your head.*

MAY

MONDAY	TUESDAY	WEDNESDAY	THURSDAY	FRIDAY	SATURDAY	SUNDAY
			1	2	3	4
5	6	7	8	9	10	11
12	13	14	15	16	17	18
19	20	21	22	23	24	25
26	27	28	29	30	31	

Check back on your Bliss List goals, stepping stones, and your 101 Things list. What are you going to make a priority this month? What will you do to take you a step closer to where you want to be? Is there anything new you need to add this month?

My Goals	By When?	Done ✓

Am I in alignment with these goals?

What may block me achieving them this month, and what I can do about it?

What resources or help will I need?

Use this page to note all the little things, and the big things that you need to do, remember, schedule or make time for this month.

Things to Do:

Things to Remember / Schedule:

Ways to Treasure Myself:

MONTHLY MANIFESTATION

What do you want to create in your life this month? A pay rise, a proposal, an unexpected gift, a new soulful friend, new shoes, a green smoothie, a parking space at work? Have fun with it. Remember, the universe delights in bringing you gifts. But first, you must place your order. Do so here. Be as specific as you can: the more detail you use, the more you fine-tune your ability to attract all you desire.

MY BLISSED MONTH ORDER

EVERYTHING I'M GRATEFUL FOR THIS MONTH

JUNE

Believe in yourself. Sometimes we know we're on the right path when our fear is the greatest.

JUNE

MONDAY	TUESDAY	WEDNESDAY	THURSDAY	FRIDAY	SATURDAY	SUNDAY
30						1
2	3	4	5	6	7	8
9	10	11	12	13	14	15
16	17	18	19	20	21	22
23	24	25	26	27	28	29

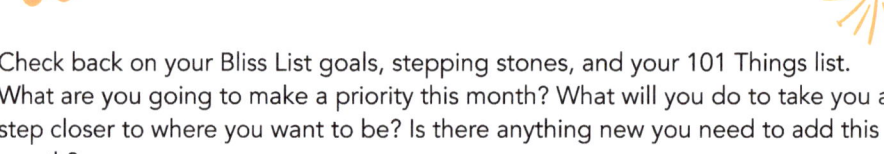

Check back on your Bliss List goals, stepping stones, and your 101 Things list. What are you going to make a priority this month? What will you do to take you a step closer to where you want to be? Is there anything new you need to add this month?

My Goals	By When?	Done ✓

Am I in alignment with these goals?

What may block me achieving them this month, and what I can do about it?

What resources or help will I need?

Use this page to note all the little things, and the big things that you need to do, remember, schedule or make time for this month.

Things to Do:

Things to Remember / Schedule:

Ways to Treasure Myself:

MONTHLY MANIFESTATION

What do you want to create in your life this month? A pay rise, a proposal, an unexpected gift, a new soulful friend, new shoes, a green smoothie, a parking space at work? Have fun with it. Remember, the universe delights in bringing you gifts. But first, you must place your order. Do so here. Be as specific as you can: the more detail you use, the more you fine-tune your ability to attract all you desire.

MY BLISSED MONTH ORDER

EVERYTHING I'M GRATEFUL FOR THIS MONTH

JULY

Treating yourself is an essential expression of self-love.

JULY

MONDAY	TUESDAY	WEDNESDAY	THURSDAY	FRIDAY	SATURDAY	SUNDAY
	1	2	3	4	5	6
7	8	9	10	11	12	13
14	15	16	17	18	19	20
21	22	23	24	25	26	27
28	29	30	31			

Check back on your Bliss List goals, stepping stones, and your 101 Things list. What are you going to make a priority this month? What will you do to take you a step closer to where you want to be? Is there anything new you need to add this month?

My Goals	By When?	Done ✓

Am I in alignment with these goals?

What may block me achieving them this month, and what I can do about it?

What resources or help will I need?

Use this page to note all the little things, and the big things that you need to do, remember, schedule or make time for this month.

Things to Do:

Things to Remember / Schedule:

Ways to Treasure Myself:

MONTHLY MANIFESTATION

What do you want to create in your life this month? A pay rise, a proposal, an unexpected gift, a new soulful friend, new shoes, a green smoothie, a parking space at work? Have fun with it. Remember, the universe delights in bringing you gifts. But first, you must place your order. Do so here. Be as specific as you can: the more detail you use, the more you fine-tune your ability to attract all you desire.

MY BLISSED MONTH ORDER

EVERYTHING I'M GRATEFUL FOR THIS MONTH

AUGUST

Begin before you are ready.
You don't have to have it all worked
out to move forward.

AUGUST

MONDAY	TUESDAY	WEDNESDAY	THURSDAY	FRIDAY	SATURDAY	SUNDAY
				1	2	3
4	5	6	7	8	9	10
11	12	13	14	15	16	17
18	19	20	21	22	23	24
25	26	27	28	29	30	31

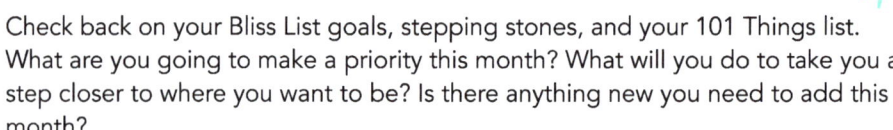

Check back on your Bliss List goals, stepping stones, and your 101 Things list. What are you going to make a priority this month? What will you do to take you a step closer to where you want to be? Is there anything new you need to add this month?

My Goals	By When?	Done ✓

Am I in alignment with these goals?

What may block me achieving them this month, and what I can do about it?

What resources or help will I need?

Use this page to note all the little things, and the big things that you need to do, remember, schedule or make time for this month.

Things to Do:

Things to Remember / Schedule:

Ways to Treasure Myself:

MONTHLY MANIFESTATION

What do you want to create in your life this month? A pay rise, a proposal, an unexpected gift, a new soulful friend, new shoes, a green smoothie, a parking space at work? Have fun with it. Remember, the universe delights in bringing you gifts. But first, you must place your order. Do so here. Be as specific as you can: the more detail you use, the more you fine-tune your ability to attract all you desire.

MY BLISSED MONTH ORDER

EVERYTHING I'M GRATEFUL FOR THIS MONTH

SEPTEMBER

Sometimes you have to let go of everything you think you are to become who you're meant to be.

SEPTEMBER

MONDAY	TUESDAY	WEDNESDAY	THURSDAY	FRIDAY	SATURDAY	SUNDAY
1	2	3	4	5	6	7
8	9	10	11	12	13	14
15	16	17	18	19	20	21
22	23	24	25	26	27	28
29	30					

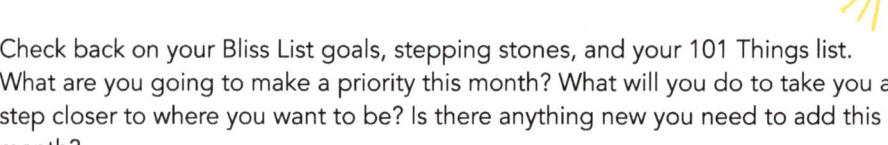

Check back on your Bliss List goals, stepping stones, and your 101 Things list. What are you going to make a priority this month? What will you do to take you a step closer to where you want to be? Is there anything new you need to add this month?

My Goals	By When?	Done

Am I in alignment with these goals?

What may block me achieving them this month, and what I can do about it?

What resources or help will I need?

Use this page to note all the little things, and the big things that you need to do, remember, schedule or make time for this month.

Things to Do:

Things to Remember / Schedule:

Ways to Treasure Myself:

MONTHLY MANIFESTATION

What do you want to create in your life this month? A pay rise, a proposal, an unexpected gift, a new soulful friend, new shoes, a green smoothie, a parking space at work? Have fun with it. Remember, the universe delights in bringing you gifts. But first, you must place your order. Do so here. Be as specific as you can: the more detail you use, the more you fine-tune your ability to attract all you desire.

MY BLISSED MONTH ORDER

EVERYTHING I'M GRATEFUL FOR THIS MONTH

OCTOBER

Follow your bliss and magic happens.

OCTOBER

MONDAY	TUESDAY	WEDNESDAY	THURSDAY	FRIDAY	SATURDAY	SUNDAY
		1	2	3	4	5
6	7	8	9	10	11	12
13	14	15	16	17	18	19
20	21	22	23	24	25	26
27	28	29	30	31		

Check back on your Bliss List goals, stepping stones, and your 101 Things list. What are you going to make a priority this month? What will you do to take you a step closer to where you want to be? Is there anything new you need to add this month?

My Goals	By When?	Done ✓

Am I in alignment with these goals?

What may block me achieving them this month, and what I can do about it?

What resources or help will I need?

Use this page to note all the little things, and the big things that you need to do, remember, schedule or make time for this month.

Things to Do:

Things to Remember / Schedule:

Ways to Treasure Myself:

MONTHLY MANIFESTATION

What do you want to create in your life this month? A pay rise, a proposal, an unexpected gift, a new soulful friend, new shoes, a green smoothie, a parking space at work? Have fun with it. Remember, the universe delights in bringing you gifts. But first, you must place your order. Do so here. Be as specific as you can: the more detail you use, the more you fine-tune your ability to attract all you desire.

MY BLISSED MONTH ORDER

EVERYTHING I'M GRATEFUL FOR THIS MONTH

NOVEMBER

*You are who you decide to be.
Choose true.*

NOVEMBER

MONDAY	TUESDAY	WEDNESDAY	THURSDAY	FRIDAY	SATURDAY	SUNDAY
					1	2
3	4	5	6	7	8	9
10	11	12	13	14	15	16
17	18	19	20	21	22	23
24	25	26	27	28	29	30

Check back on your Bliss List goals, stepping stones, and your 101 Things list. What are you going to make a priority this month? What will you do to take you a step closer to where you want to be? Is there anything new you need to add this month?

My Goals	By When?	Done

Am I in alignment with these goals?

What may block me achieving them this month, and what I can do about it?

What resources or help will I need?

Use this page to note all the little things, and the big things that you need to do, remember, schedule or make time for this month.

Things to Do:

Things to Remember / Schedule:

Ways to Treasure Myself:

MONTHLY MANIFESTATION

What do you want to create in your life this month? A pay rise, a proposal, an unexpected gift, a new soulful friend, new shoes, a green smoothie, a parking space at work? Have fun with it. Remember, the universe delights in bringing you gifts. But first, you must place your order. Do so here. Be as specific as you can: the more detail you use, the more you fine-tune your ability to attract all you desire.

MY BLISSED MONTH ORDER

EVERYTHING I'M GRATEFUL FOR THIS MONTH

DECEMBER

Sometimes, all you need to do is ... be

DECEMBER

MONDAY	TUESDAY	WEDNESDAY	THURSDAY	FRIDAY	SATURDAY	SUNDAY
1	2	3	4	5	6	7
8	9	10	11	12	13	14
15	16	17	18	19	20	21
22	23	24	25	26	27	28
29	30	31				

Check back on your Bliss List goals, stepping stones, and your 101 Things list. What are you going to make a priority this month? What will you do to take you a step closer to where you want to be? Is there anything new you need to add this month?

My Goals	By When?	Done ✓

Am I in alignment with these goals?

What may block me achieving them this month, and what I can do about it?

What resources or help will I need?

Use this page to note all the little things, and the big things that you need to do, remember, schedule or make time for this month.

Things to Do:

Things to Remember / Schedule:

Ways to Treasure Myself:

MONTHLY MANIFESTATION

What do you want to create in your life this month? A pay rise, a proposal, an unexpected gift, a new soulful friend, new shoes, a green smoothie, a parking space at work? Have fun with it. Remember, the universe delights in bringing you gifts. But first, you must place your order. Do so here. Be as specific as you can: the more detail you use, the more you fine-tune your ability to attract all you desire.

MY BLISSED MONTH ORDER

EVERYTHING I'M GRATEFUL FOR THIS MONTH

MY NEXT BEAUTIFUL YEAR

Use this space to capture your thoughts, dreams, ideas, and plans for the year to come.

YOUR SOUL WHISPERS:

I believe in you.
You are beautiful.
You are talented.
You are special.
You are perfect.
You can do this.
Just believe in you too.
Now is your time.

Believing

NOTES

Believe in yourself. You can do this.

NOTES

Believe in yourself.
You can do this.

NOTES

Believe in yourself.
You can do this.

NOTES

Believe in yourself.
You can do this.

ABOUT THE AUTHOR

Marnie McDermott is an award-winning author, heart-fuelled lifestyle coach and host of MarnieTV. Think of her as your crystal-toting, fashion-loving, spiritually-savvy soul sister, giving you the tools, tips and know-how to live your happiest life.

As the founder of marniemcdermott.com, Marnie has worked with women from all corners of the globe to create their own version of wholehearted bliss.

Her work incorporates powerful tools and programs focused on spirit-centred living, happiness, life purpose, soul, meditation, abundance, order and harmony, home, relationships, health and wellbeing, and more.

Marnie's books are hailed as the perfect blend of modern wisdom and practical know-how. Her debut book, *Beyond Happiness: The 12 Principles of Enduring Bliss*, has been internationally acclaimed as a top mind-body-spirit read, winning three awards in 2013: the National Indie Excellence Awards, the Living Now Book Awards, and recognition at the London Book Festival. Touted as 'life-changing' and 'bursting with great insight and inspiration', it shows you how to stop settling for fleeting happiness and instead unlock all the deep-down, lasting fulfilment you want and deserve. Marnie's second book, *Soul Happiness*, will be released in 2014.

www.marniemcdermott.com

www.ingramcontent.com/pod-product-compliance
Lightning Source LLC
Chambersburg PA
CBHW041611220426
43668CB00001B/8